THANK YOU FOR YOUR PURCHASE.

SCAN HERE

FOR

YOUR GIFT

Find us on

WWW.KIOSK-2000.COM

100

Funny Stories
for the
Elderly

*Large print, easy-to-read, short paragraphs,
perfect to stimulate memory*

KIOSK 2000

Contents

Introduction

Everyone gets confused. That feeling of not knowing what to do because nothing makes sense is quite common. But as you grow older, this confused feeling of yours might increase. It might annoy or even anger you, and sometimes, when you can't handle what you are feeling, you lash out. Or maybe someone else will lash out at you, getting upset over the confusion and chaos. But it's okay to feel frustrated when things get out of control.

My own experience taking care of my elderly mother has taught me that it isn't your fault, and it isn't their fault either. Living with her and engaging with people who go through what she does, I have come to realize that we must look past the memory and embrace the individual spirit that dwells within us. And that's what you will be doing while reading this book.

This book can help you ease that frustration you might be feeling. By making you laugh, it could also help increase the blood flow in your brain and promote memory function. So hopefully, you won't be forgetting where you kept those glasses anytime soon.

These hilarious easy-to-digest stories will not only be relatable but will also help to reflect on the wonderful memories that you've experienced and recall all the loved friends and family that have been a part of it.

Illustrating the many challenges and setbacks that we experience in life, this book also celebrates our simple pleasures and interests. Making you laugh and smile, while also improving your mental abilities and memory.

The Twist

Hetty was hard of hearing.

"Do you have a spare cup of sugar, perchance?" Ronald shouted.

"Why on earth would I want to dance, Ronald?" she replied, quite baffled.

He wildly gesticulated and mimed writing a shopping list, "No—sugar! I forgot to put it on my shopping list!"

"I certainly do not want to do the Twist Ronald, so you can stop waving your arms about like that. You look like a lunatic."

Then, Ronald had an idea, he took Hetty's hands and started to hum a tune—which Hetty couldn't hear. But her body remembered all the moves from 1959. Together on the doorstep Ronald and Hetty silently danced the Twist. Sugar forgotten.

2

Bottoms Up

Malcolm whistled as he worked, pulling up weeds and deadheading his roses. He didn't hear beautiful Marjorie's high heels clip-clop as she walked up to his garden path.

A tough old weed was giving him trouble, refusing to budge no matter how much he heaved or sighed.

In a final heroic attempt, he bent his knees, widened his stance, and just as he heard a cheery, "Hello Malcolm, lovely day!" there was an almighty rip down the seam of his trousers, revealing his striped underwear.

Malcolm went tumbling backward, the weed flailing from his hand.

From his prostrate position on the lawn, a pretty, bespectacled face peered down at him.

"Ah Marjorie, hello. I'm just admiring the view."

3

Grandmother's Mutiny

My daughter is a slave driver. A dictator of parenting. A hater of sugar, of television, and clothes covered in mud.

We nod along, repeating the mantra: Bath time at six, bedtime by seven, no sweets or screens after five.

"Goodbye! Have fun!" We watch as she strides to her car, and whizzes off.

I close the door and turn. My charge, dear Heidi, stands in the hall, holding her doll by its leg.

She grins. I wink.

From my pocket, I pull out my hidden stash of sugary treats and I say, "let's go have some fun, little one."

4

Hair Today, Gone Tomorrow

I thanked the barber, although the fringe was wonky, and my mother would kill me.

Years later, I wept at the hair by my feet—on my wedding day. My wife never forgave me, but still, I thanked him.

My son asked me to stay in the car and that time the barber gave me highlights. "You look like a hamster has died on your head," he said.

Now, I have no use for the barber, just a cap to keep my scalp warm.

I thank him anyway.

"What for?" he asks.

"Oh, I'll never be sad like other balding men," I explained. "I'm just relieved."

5

Wandering Washing

When my underwear disappeared from the line, I thought the wind had snatched them. I hoped they didn't land in Mrs. Weaver's garden; those smalls had seen better days.

When another three pairs went wandering, I feared someone was playing tricks. I called over the fence to Mrs. Joyce, "Have your knickers gone missing too?"

But she just cried, "oh, there you are Carlos!" to the cat hiding under a bush.

Carlos meowed. I peered over the fence. The cat was curled up in my underwear, surrounded by kittens.

The mystery was solved, and Carlos's name was promptly changed to Carla.

6

The Son-in-Law

My son-in-law thinks I'm past it.

"What's the point in having a phone if it's always switched off?" he complains.

He's hired a handyman. Doesn't trust me up a ladder.

Imagine my surprise when he showed up yesterday, cheeks wet with tears. She'd left him, and wouldn't answer her phone.

My bones creaked as I sat at the desk. My hands shook as I passed him the pen. But love letters never grow old. Something, at last, that I could teach him.

Later I looked at the photo of my late wife, our love as prevalent today no matter the years that went by.

The Shape of Friendship

My best friend is forever causing trouble.

She refuses to look smart and makes a mess wherever she goes. Last week she was thrown out of our local coffee shop for upending a table. You can't take her anywhere.

Poor George almost had a heart attack yesterday, as she pawed at him and kissed his face. He'd only gone out for a newspaper.

My best friend is always by my side and loves me unconditionally.

Oh Lottie, my lovely Labrador.

She's smelly and she's clumsy. Her preferred past-time is chasing squirrels, and her favorite meal is rubbish from the trash.

I wouldn't have her any other way: my best friend, my Lottie.

The Lodger

I was afraid when I heard the scratching in the walls, the sheets pulled up to my nose.

"Who's there?"

Scratch scratch, the noise replied.

I lay awake all night, even when the noise was silent.

The following day, wrapped up in my winter coat, I looked for holes in the brickwork where naughty noises could burrow in.

I found a tiny gap and I poked it with a stick. Two tiny beady eyes appeared, before retreating, irritated to be disturbed.

"Well, now you know what it's like," I huffed.

These days we have an understanding, the bat and I. My lodger scratches goodnight, and I say "sleep well."

We dream of summer days ahead.

9

The Invisible Woman

From my armchair by the window, I watch as two policemen knock on every door except mine.

I open up my notebook. I had sketched the perpetrators of the crime two nights ago. Bravely, I'd stepped outside pretending to water my roses, and managed to catch their names.

The young scoundrels just thought I was batty, gardening in the middle of the night. They didn't lower their voices, and I heard everything. The evidence is in my hands.

Nobody hides from my gaze, I explain in the note I'll be mailing to the station.

I signed off: The Invisible Woman.

10

Felicity to the Rescue

Felicity wasn't keen on the rowboat I'd hired.

"Good lord Bernie, I barely trust you to navigate dry land."

It was my birthday, and she was too nice to refuse. Things were going swimmingly—excuse the pun—well until I lost the oar.

"Don't worry, I'll use the other oar to guide it back to us," I told her with confidence I didn't feel.

I dropped the second oar into the water and off it floated back to shore, which Felicity wished she had never left.

As she always had, as she always would, Felicity took control. Off came her summer dress, her pretty shoes, and sun hat, and in she jumped. My wife, my savior, to the rescue.

Ringo

The cleaner loathed Frank's friend.

"He's disgusting. And he's always getting under my feet."

Frank shushed her frantically, "he'll hear you!"

"Oh, I very much doubt that. He pays no attention whatsoever. Does he even have ears? Such an ugly fellow."

Frank was distraught. How could she be so cruel?

"My friend, Shirley, says he's incontinent. It's me who has to mop, remember?" the cleaner continued.

At this, Frank could take no more, Ringo wasn't a mouse. Shirley was quite mad.

He roared, "Ringo Starr is a well-respected beetle, and is very useful in the garden I'll have you know!"

Ringo nodded in appreciation and scuttled off indignantly.

12

The Wedding

"She looks splendid," somebody gushed.

She did. A gown that shimmered, revealing her delicate shoulders. Her golden curls were crowned with silver leaves.

The vicar looked more earnest than ever before. He kept clearing his throat and looking sideways. The groom urged him to go on.

He repeated his call for objections. Nobody objected this time either.

So with one final cough and a sharp intake of breath, the vicar said, "I object!"

The guests gasped, the groom raised a fist, and the bride swooned as the vicar fell to one knee, asking the bride for her hand in marriage.

She said yes.

By Hook or By Crook

He wasn't the first person to try to overtake Beatrice that afternoon.

There was the woman with the child, the man in the shiny suit, and the kissing teenagers. They'd nearly knocked her over.

Beatrice had tutted. No manners.

Slowly, she'd continued along the path, her wooden walking stick a favored friend.

She heard his labored breath first. His feet thudded fast on the ground behind her. Then further away, shouts, "'catch him, he stole my handbag!"

Beatrice had had enough. She stopped dead in her tracks and swiftly pushed out her stick.

Its hook caught the crook by his ankles and the handbag was promptly returned.

Nobody else tried to push past Beatrice that day. She was given a medal.

Road Trip

Maurice and Helena had agreed it would be nice to getaway.

"Are we nearly there yet?" chirruped one of the children.

"I need a pee!" demanded the other.

Helena sighed. Maurice pulled over. They'd been driving for less than 10 minutes.

Back on the road, they hit the highway, just another three hours to the beach. Sixteen more toilet stops later, they arrived. The sun was shining, the sea was clear blue, and the kids built castles made of sand.

"It was worth it in the end," Maurice commented on the way home. Helena smiled and yawned contentedly.

From the backseat, a voice asked, "are we nearly home yet? I need a pee." The other, with a belly full of ice cream, cried, "I think I'm going to be sick!'

A Flutter

He was running late. He forgot to tie his shoelaces and tripped as he ran for the bus. The bus drove off. It started to rain.

Cold, wet, with a hole in his trousers, the graze on his knee was dripping blood. As he walked, the wind picked up and blew the cap from his head.

They didn't call him 'Unlucky Hugh' for nothing.

He had a wager on a horse and he was due a change in luck.

He cheered and shouted as the horse fell to second place, third place, then last. He couldn't watch, so he covered his eyes and walked away.

"Ouch!" cried the lady he bumped into.

He looked at the voice and smiled at the woman who would become his wife.

"Looks like my luck has just changed, after all."

16

Love Letters

This is a love letter to number nine. I hope your interview went well and this envelope contains a job.

This is a love letter to the lady at number 12. I bet this is the parcel you've been waiting for, a photograph of your grandchild enclosed.

This is a love letter to the bright young man at number 16. I've been praying that your college application was successful. This envelope has the school's motto on the back.

The rain on my face, the dog at my heels, the ache in my legs. Nothing will stop me from delivering your news, your family, your opportunities, and more, all to your door.

This is a love letter from me, your mailman, to you.

Poker Face

"How are the grandchildren Fred?" Josephine politely inquired as she picked a card from the stack.

"Very well, thank you for asking." Fred laid his card and sweetly smiled.

"You do look well Hilda," Josephine said, "have you done something different to your hair?"

She took another card and set her hand down. "Oh you are too kind," replied Hilda.

Josephine studied the cards fanned in her palm and frowned. Distracted, she pointed at the window, "oh look, a bluebird in the tree!"

And as Fred and Hilda turned away to see the bird, Josephine slipped the ace from her sleeve and into her hand.

She'd won again.

18

An Argument

"You snore."

"You take up the whole bed!"

"You leave wet towels on the bathroom floor."

"You leave crumbs on the countertop!"

"You never take the trash out."

"You never say you love me!"

"Oh but I do, love you, I mean."

"And I, you, you silly old man."

"Shall we carry on, then? Living here, annoying each other?"

"Oh yes, there's nothing I'd like more."

19

Swimming Lesson

The water looked inviting from where she sat on the riverbank. Its ripples glistened; golden little fish squirmed beneath.

Shoes and socks discarded, her toes played with the blades of grass, cooling on the dewdrops.

So hot, so stifling. Would it hurt to have a little dip? She knew what her mother would say.

Not caring a bit, she whipped off her clothes and hung them in a tree. The water was glorious! Splashing and swimming and floating, staring up at the clouds.

The magpie took his chance as she dived below, snatching the items she'd left strewn across the branches. His nest would be the envy of all.

20

The Stowaway in the Shed

Mary was perplexed. She had bought a bag of carrots and some cabbage, but it had vanished. The next day she went to the grocery store and bought more fresh vegetables. By dinnertime, they'd disappeared again.

Mary cried to Peter, "that's all the money gone this week!"

Mary had a restless night and was woken up early by the sound of children's commotion in the yard. She peered out of the window and saw a queue of 30 children, coins jingling in hand.

Running downstairs, she shouted, "Peter, what's going on?"

She stopped, suddenly, as she saw her husband leading a long-haired donkey, with two children on its back, down the garden path.

"Honest Mary, I just found him hiding in the shed, but I took pity on him and fed him all your vegetables, and now, I told him he'll have to earn his keep!"

The Pianist

Did I ever tell you about the pianist? He was a funny old fellow. He played 100 miles per hour for 13 hours a day, only stopping to eat some peanut butter on bread.

He was 72 when I met him, and he said to me, "I'm old now Jeremy, and I've never left this town."

The pianist craved adventure. Up a mountain, he wanted to go. I was a little concerned, but he was not to be deterred.

I arrived with a map, and he'd packed his peanut butter and bread. His piano was strapped to some old skis, the rope tied around his waist.

Up we trundled, piano and all. Eventually, we reached the top. And the pianist played, and the birds sang along for a while.

22

Camping Holiday

"See, I told you it would be fun," Geoffrey said to Celia, as they drank tea on the grass. They put the sausages on the stove to cook and took a stroll around the lake.

"What the—'"

The couple ran back towards the tent where two raccoons were enjoying the feast, one sat on the deckchair, the other wearing Celia's hat.

"Shoo!" they shouted, the raccoons looked affronted.

The furry friends finished their feast, and returned the hat, thinking, *how very rude.*

As Geoffrey and Celia lay hungry that night, a sudden gust of wind ripped their shelter straight out of the ground.

"I told you it wouldn't be fun," said Celia, as her husband chased the flying tent through a field.

Fisherman

He had sat on the bank for hours when he felt the rod tug. A bite!

He pulled himself tall and started to wind. But the reel wouldn't wind and the rod dragged the fisherman towards the edge.

Heave ho! He dug in his heels and leaned back, straining with all his might. In return, the rod didn't budge.

Suddenly, something gave and came loose. Waves appeared, and the water clouded. A final fight. Breathless, the fisherman grunted, using all his strength.

Out from the water, the huge and heavy creature emerged: An old bicycle, rusty and worn.

24

The Disappearing Popsicle

When I was a girl, I couldn't resist a popsicle. Nothing much has changed. They've taken us out for a day at the seaside, and I've already eaten two.

"Time to get back on the bus!" the woman commands us, although I'm twice her age.

The others shuffle obediently in line. I have time for one more, a red one that tastes of cherry.

I'm quicker than you'd think, I dart to the cart and hide my frozen treat in my pocket. She doesn't allow food on the bus.

I decided to wait until the others have nodded off to eat it; I don't intend to share. Then I reach for my prize, deep into my pocket. But all I find is a wooden stick, and a cold wet patch on my dress.

Fireworks

It was love at first sight for Richard. Not so much for Geraldine. Each day, he'd say, "you're beautiful."

"Fiddlesticks!" Geraldine would reply.

He brought her fresh flowers, but still, she said no. "We're far too old to be courting," she'd admonished.

One night, awoken by a racket, Geraldine peered from her window. Richard stood surrounded by candles, and string lights. He started to serenade her.

Geraldine hadn't been serenaded before, let alone by a mad man in a dressing gown in the middle of the night.

The rain started to fall, the candles were extinguished, and the bulbs began to pop. Richard sang on.

And as the final light fizzled out, the fireworks finally began.

26

Drive-In Date

I am running late when Brad rings the bell to pick me up. It's my parents' fault for going out. Usually, Mom helps me with my curls and irons my blouse.

Brad waits while I fix my hair. When we arrive at the drive-in it's packed full, so we have to park behind another car.

As if the night couldn't get any worse, the couple in front start kissing, their bobbing heads distracting us from the movie.

When I can take no more, I jump out of Brad's car and storm to theirs, rapping on the window.

The couple stops kissing and wind down the window.

"Dad? Mom?"

My parents smooth down their ruffled hair and smile, "hello darling," they say, "it's date night for us too."

Regrets

I have a few regrets, but I don't regret you.

Like that time I climbed the apple tree, the branch snapped, and I fell. The other kids laughed, but you held out your hand and brushed me off.

I have a few regrets, but I don't regret you.

Like that time I forgot to fill the tank and the car ran out of gas. We were late for our engagement party. Your mother was furious, but you held out your hand, and we danced.

I have a few regrets, but I don't regret you.

Like that time we argued. Like that time I forgot our anniversary. Like that time I didn't say I love you. But you always held out your hand. You always held mine.

The Explorers

Terence studied his map, brow furrowed.

"Are we lost, Dad?"

Terence shook his head, "Of course not James, we're just exploring."

The four explorers bravely continued up the hill to the horizon, beyond which they found another horizon, and another after that.

"Are you sure we're not lost, Dad?"

"Juliette, I'd factored in at least eight horizons before lunchtime."

Onward they marched, as the day drew on and the sun dipped beneath the 11th horizon of the day.

As dusk passed, and the moon settled in, Terence whispered to his wife, "dearest, I think we may be lost."

The Interview

They asked me why I wanted the job. I'd practiced the right answer in the mirror that morning, but it had gone clean out of my head.

"It's the only one available," I replied, "'and I'm pretty desperate."

The gray-haired man in the bright purple tie glared and scribbled furiously in his pad.

He wanted to know where I saw myself in a year.

"Anywhere but this awful hell-hole," I quipped, promptly realizing that was the wrong answer too.

He bristled then politely inquired about my best quality.

Now, that one I knew. "Honesty, sir," I told him, "I simply can't tell a lie."

30

Wasps' Nest

The wasps moved in on Tuesday. By lunchtime, they had made themselves at home. They lounged on the sofa and slept in the beds. They sunned themselves on window sills and cooled down on the kitchen tiles.

"Ouch!" everyone said, rubbing lotion on their stings. Elbows, necks, and bottoms too.

By Thursday, David had a plan. He found their nest in the garage wall, and therefore located their queen. He filled up his petrol can, and he poured it all in. He lit a match.

David watched from the street, pleased with himself, eviction complete. The nest exploded, and the queen was gone.

Then the whole garage fell.

31

New Year's Eve

Five, four, three, two, one! The midnight bell chimed and the party cheered, the women in sequins and the men looking smart.

The fireworks exploded, the lights went off.

In the darkness, Ruby sought out her husband for a midnight kiss, but instead, she found Joe. Her husband accidentally kissed Ray.

Lizzie kissed Fran, and George kissed the dog, who had jumped up from under the table.

The blackout ended, the lights came on. The party all went quite red.

"I'm sorry."

"No, *I'm* sorry," they all said.

Then they laughed, and never spoke of it again.

32

The Student

In her 69th year, Dolores decided it was time for a change.

She couldn't wait to tell the kids her news. Her son picked her up at five, and the whole family sat down for dinner at six.

Dolores explained her plans, and that babysitting duties would cease, "I start next Tuesday," she said.

Her daughter-in-law was aghast. She sent the children to their rooms. Her son dropped his fork, and a pea rolled onto the floor.

"What on earth do you need to go to college for?" he asked.

"Well, my darling," Dolores told him, "you can't do anything without a degree these days."

33

Toddler's Truth

The chicken was in the oven, and Margaret and Susan were chatting. Roger and Roy talked politics. Susan's young daughter played contentedly at their feet.

"Oh isn't she just a dear," people always said, admiring her pretty dresses and her angelic smile.

When the doorbell rang, Margaret jumped to her feet.

"Hello Pat, do come in!"

In waddled Pat, quite out of breath, her dress stretched tight around her oversized bosom.

"Why is that lady so fat?" asked the angelic small child.

"Yes! That lady is called Pat!" they all shouted too loud, before ushering Pat to the kitchen.

34

Bubblegum

Rachel had the most beautiful hair. Caramel in color, waves like the sea. It was her pride and joy, and all the other girls envied it.

Unfortunately, that was the only nice thing about her.

"You look like a boy," she spat at Loulou, "your hair is so short, and your hips too narrow." Rachel stuck out her tongue, placed a piece of bubblegum on it, and blew a bubble bigger than her head.

Loulou blinked back her tears and stood tall. She would take this bullying no more! With her little finger, she popped the huge bubble, and it exploded all over Rachel's perfect hair.

35

Dentist's Chair

Gerald had been dreading this day all year. He brushed twice a day and flossed. He boasted to his friends that he was the only one among them who still had his teeth.

On this day, it was different. His friends smirked and grinned, revealing their bright white false teeth.

He shook as he took the chair, the dentist a menace above him, armed with whirring metal contraptions full of sharp edges; a clear threat.

"No!" he protested, "please, no!"

The coat-wearing pest placed down his instruments, and instead offered the gas. Gerald took it with glee and didn't stop laughing all day.

36

Wedding Crashers

We couldn't believe our luck when the invitations arrived. We talked of nothing else, but when the bride walked past and greeted the boss with a kiss, we were silent.

"Daddy," she might say, "I've decided on pink roses after all."

We'd make notes in our minds about what to wear. Her dress had 1,000 beads, all stitched by hand.

Yet on the wedding day, we missed the bus and had to run all the way. From the back pew, we saw a vision in white standing at the altar, a tall man by her side.

Ready to cheer when they turned to the crowd, imagine the shock we all felt when it wasn't Christina we saw. We'd gatecrashed the wedding next door.

Grocery Store

Wilma's basket was full as she headed to the checkout.

As she reached the front of the line, she placed her basket on the belt, noting the absence of staff.

"Remove items from the bagging area," a disembodied voice said.

Wilma was getting quite cross, "where are you?" she asked.

No answer came. The belt didn't move. A red light on the screen flashed. Wilma tried to reason with it, "could I speak with the manager?" she said.

Eventually, the robotic voice returned, asking for the next customer, please.

Wilma, now furious, abandoned her basket and left.

38

Memories

"Mom, this place is too big for you now," my daughter said.

She's right, always is. She takes after me.

My home for 54 years is more than just bricks. There are three children and five grandkids. My closet is full of dresses I no longer wear. I like them; they remind me of me.

This place, far too large, is not just my shelter. It is lined on the wall as they get tall, and pictures they drew on the fridge.

Memories, photo albums, trinkets, and dust.

I place the Retirement Village brochure in the middle drawer. My daughter knows best, but I know much more. This place is my life, the best one I've got, too big or not.

39

Fairground

I had a mouth full of cotton candy when Scott said hello. I tried to reply, but a muffled sound came out instead, from behind my pink, sticky teeth. I was mortified, and my friends giggled.

We played hook-a-duck, and I won a huge cuddly bear. On the carousel, we raced and made up names for our horses. Mine was called Rose, though Scott said he looked more like a Ralph.

On the big wheel, right at the top, as we gently rocked in time to the breeze, Scott asked me to go steady. I said okay, and the car seemed to reach the stars.

40

Night at the Opera

My son has done very well for himself. He eats food with names I can't pronounce and vacations in the Hamptons.

For my birthday, he bought me tickets to the opera and I invited my friend Jeannie. We've lived 68 years and never once gone. He said that wouldn't do.

A pretty dress, some lipstick, and off we went. Never too late to try something new.

The costumes were beautiful, and the seats were comfortable. The binoculars made us laugh. But we didn't understand a word of it, so we left at the intermission and went to the movies instead.

Hotel Room

Crisp white sheets were cool against her skin. Caro stretched on the enormous bed, thinking of last night. The sparkling chandeliers, the shiny ballroom floor. Her dress shimmered as she danced.

She couldn't sleep, she needed a pee. Caro got up and found her bathroom door. It swung shut behind her.

The light from the large window illuminated the corridor. Caro was not in her en-suite, but had walked straight out of her room and into the hall.

She heard a porter whistle, the wheels of his trolley squeaked. She was naked as the day she was born. Frantically, Caro unhooked the curtain from the window and wrapped it around herself, just in time.

42

Game of Chess

I don't watch television during the day, I'm no couch potato, retired or not. Instead, I play chess against the computer and listen to the radio to keep up with the news.

There is a call-in talk show on. I listen to the oldies moan about this and that. I feel sorry for them; they must be bored.

The computer is losing, again. I move my bishop. His king is in danger.

Kathy from Delaware is talking about how everything was better when she was young.

Nonsense, I think, as I take my final turn. Checkmate. You couldn't play chess with the computer in our day.

43

Motorcycle Man

It was nine a.m. on Sunday morning so William was where he always was at that time; in his garage, tinkering with his motorcycle.

That's what his wife called it—*tinkering*. William wasn't tinkering, he was fine-tuning. He had been for years.

"Are you ever going to get the engine going?" she asked.

Today, William believed he would.

Final adjustments made, he finished polishing the fender. He turned the key, and there was a mighty roar!

His wife came running out, and the neighbors all watched from their yards. William jumped aboard and felt the wind in his face as everyone cheered. His motorcycle was alive once again!

The Community Garden

'Welcome to the Community Garden,' the sign said, 'A Place for Friends.'

The friends were warming up in the shed, discussing the size of their zucchini.

"I highly doubt yours is bigger than mine!" Shirley was indignant and already crossed paths with George, who she suspected had hidden her best spade.

The friends, you see, were fierce rivals.

"Neither of you has a chance at beating me!" chipped in Frank, who had sabotaged Rita's carrots last week.

Betty arrived, holding a zucchini twice the size of any they'd ever seen.

The friends united and said in chorus, "oh look she's such a big cheat!"

Picnic in the Snow

Since my twin sister and I were eight years old, we have always had the first picnic of the year on our birthday, April 10th.

That year we were determined it would be no different, despite the freak fall of heavy springtime snow.

Our friends declined to join us, saying we were mad, we'd freeze. The weather was so bad.

"No such thing as bad weather," we'd haughtily informed them, "only unsuitable clothing." Our father had taught us this, and we were hardy women.

Just the two of us sat on three blankets piled up, and ate sandwiches wearing our gloves, as snowflakes fell into our lemonade.

We agreed, it was the best birthday picnic yet.

46

The Audition

My knees were knocking as I stood in line on stage. Choir practice was on Tuesday at 11 a.m., I'd miss double math if I could get in.

The choir wasn't a popular club, unlike soccer or drama, and so the line was meager in size.

Ms. Winterbottom stood stern in front of us. Each child took a turn to sing.

"Soprano."

"Tenor."

"Mezzo."

"Bass."

She moved us like chess pieces as she selected our place.

It was my turn to sing, and I can't sing a note, but still, I gave it my best. She stepped back in horror, lips pursed in displeasure. She needed the numbers, though perhaps not my voice.

"Groaner," she stated matter of factly and asked me to mime at the back.

Portrait of a Lady

Harriet was using the artist's dog as a footstool. He didn't dare complain. Harriet was formidable.

"You look very beautiful, ma'am," said her housekeeper nervously, and she did. Her dark hair shone, her skin glowed. She had excellent bone structure.

"'No one asked you," Harriet replied, "now fetch some coffee."

She complained at the light, of a stiff back, and the artist taking too long. She threatened to sack him eight times.

Eventually, he finished. Harriet gasped when she saw her likeness, for it wasn't like her at all. A monster stared back from the canvas.

"I've captured your inner beauty," the artist said, and the housekeeper stifled a smile.

Flirtation

Dennis took a seat at the bar next to the beautiful woman with long gray hair.

"May I get you a drink?" he asked, "what's your name?"

She smiled, he was handsome and the lines on his face spoke of a lifetime of laughter.

"Valerie," she said shyly and held out her hand. He took a risk, and rather than take it or shake it, he gently kissed her long, slender fingers.

She didn't pull away.

They drank a bottle of wine and talked of everything and nothing. Last orders came, but Dennis and Valerie weren't finished. The flirtation continued.

Before leaving, Dennis said, "dear Valerie, my organs may be failing but I would be happy to give you my heart," Valerie chuckled.

And three months later, they were married.

49

The Birthday Party

John and Sarah arrived early. The banner read "Happy 40th Birthday."

"That can't be right," remarked John, "it was just yesterday she couldn't ride a bike."

Sarah, just as surprised as her husband, replied, "nevermind yesterday, it was only last week she weighed 10 pounds."

They watched guests arrive; friends, colleagues, and cousins.

"Remember her first date?" John prompted woefully, he hadn't liked that.

"The time she dyed her hair?" Sarah chuckled, recalling the mess.

"When she passed her exams? She was always smart," John proudly said.

"Her wedding day? She was beautiful," Sarah wiped away a tear.

"She still is," replied John, smiling as their daughter, Emma, walked towards them. John and Sarah held out their arms welcoming their precious daughter. Four decades of precious memories, with plenty more to come.

While in their arms, Emma whispered, "Mom, Dad, can I ask you something?"

"Why, of course," John replied, "what is it, precious?"

With a heavy sigh, Sarah said, "I love you guys so much, but you do know that I am only 30 right?"

50

There's Always a Way

"I don't feel well," Arthur whined. "I can't find my shoe," he continued.

The excuses were endless, but his mom simply said, "you are going to school, however, you feel, with or without your left shoe."

The boy sulked until they arrived at the bridge they had to cross on the way to school. Suddenly the boy perked up—an act of god for sure, he thought. The bridge had tumbled down in the rain!

His mom, who had lived here for years, was always prepared. She pulled something from her backpack and blew it up until it became an inflatable boat.

"If you get it," she told her son, "there's always a way to school."

Holiday

I can't wait for my holiday. I pack my suitcase, check my tickets, and head to the airport. I was excited to escape my life for a little while.

The plane is delayed, and the air-conditioner is fierce. It's much too humid when we arrive. My room is too small, with no sea view. I don't like the food.

Sat on my deck chair, I hear children play. I've gotten used to the food, and the room is quite cozy now. Yesterday, I even made a friend.

We eat dinner together and watch the sunset. We talk of our homes and our families. She, like me, couldn't wait for her holiday as well. But unlike me, she likes her small room with no sea view. Also, she loves the food.

"What a wonderful time I've had," she told me last night.

"Me too," I concede, "but now I can't wait to go home."

52

Tap Dance

Sam turned off the television. Trixie was usually home by now. The next day, she was late again, carrying a bag concealed behind her.

"Where have you been?" he asked.

"Nowhere," she lied.

Later, he snooped and found a silver dress covered in sequins. His 70th birthday party was on Saturday and Trixie was off gallivanting, up to no good.

The night of the party arrived, and Sam was feeling glum. He couldn't see Trixie anywhere. The music stopped. Suddenly she appeared under a spotlight, shining like a star.

"Darling Sam, my gift to you: I've learned to tap dance your favorite tune!"

The crowd cheered and Trixie made Sam the proudest man in the room.

53

Ghost Story

A ghost moved in last week. At first, I thought it was an intruder, which would have been worse. You never know what you're going to get with an intruder.

Once I'd realized there was no one in the house but me, the ghosts—there were two of them now—started to keep me company.

One of them took a keen interest in baseball and kept me up to date on the scores. Enormously helpful chap.

I was listening in on their conversation when I noticed the curtain fluttering. I pulled it back and was faced with my mistake.

There was no ghost, just my trusty old radio, concealed behind the drapes.

Pie Maker

Doris had lost her marbles, they said.

The store clerk had sold her three baskets full of groceries, far too much for one woman and her cat.

Someone rang her daughter, who promised to check in. When she arrived Doris was frantically baking, surrounded by steaming hot pies.

"Oh, Mother!" she cried.

The nosy neighbors were hovering outside.

"Oh I'm glad you're all here," said Doris, quite sane, "here, help me carry some pies."

Not daring to argue, they followed Doris as she led them to the homeless shelter and fed the veterans, bag ladies, and all those who had lost their way.

"Same time next week?" Doris asked her helpers, with a wink.

Librarian

"Shhhhh," the librarian pursed her lips and wagged her finger, "no talking please," she crossly said.

The girls zipped their lips but giggled as soon as her back was turned.

The librarian made a sign. *Silence please.* As she pinned it to the noticeboard, a young man praised her efforts.

"That includes you!" she roared. "Shhhhhh."

The man backed away.

All day the librarian shouted at those who broke the rules. They were spoiling it for everyone else.

After her shift, she was just closing up when her manager called her over for a word.

"I'm afraid I'll have to let you go," he said, "for making too much noise."

56

The Concert

Toby played the trombone and he was marvelous. The breath from his lungs and the magic in his fingers created a wonderful sound.

But tonight he was nervous, butterflies dancing in his stomach. Carla was coming to watch. Toby adored her.

Bossy Fran next door had asked her along. Fran had bad breath and didn't make him nervous at all.

He saw Carla in the audience, as though she was the one in the spotlight, and began his solo.

The butterflies flapped harder and harder, but he still blew.

The long deep tone emerged from the brass bell, just at the same time as a gentle, but audible 'toot!' from his bottom.

Art Class

The teacher was getting impatient. Her elderly evening class was harder to manage than the children.

"Harry, please stop looking out of the window and take your seat at the front," she commanded, but Harry wouldn't turn around.

"Vera and Poppy, please do stop whispering and giggling! I'm sure you've seen it all before."

Each of her pupils was acting the clown. Not sitting down, laughing, and talking. One red-faced man had walked straight out.

Apart from Lizzie, who was looking earnestly at the model. Finally, one who is grown-up enough to take still life drawing seriously, the teacher thought.

Then Lizzie brazenly asked him out.

The Newspaper

Shelley searched for it everywhere and couldn't find it.

She asked her granddaughter, "do you know where the newspaper is?"

Her granddaughter looked back, thoroughly shocked. Was the question that absurd?

After a moment's pause, she said, "Grandma, this is the 21st century!"

"So?"

Exasperated, she replied, "why would I waste money on newspapers if my iPad can provide it?"

Then she handed over her iPad saying, "you can use this instead."

Shelley looked down at the iPad and sighed, "flies can be swatted with iPads now?" Every day you learn something new.

59

The Talking Frog

Henry is 68 years old. Henry goes fishing every weekend. Henry loves fishing.

One day, to everyone's surprise, he came back with a frog. To top it off, he was talking to the frog. Is Henry alright?

Concerned, we asked him why he was talking to the frog. Before he could respond, we heard someone say, "I want him to kiss me."

Who said that? Where did that voice come from?

"I am here," the voice said. It came from Henry's pocket.

"Meet Violet," Henry said, pointing to the frog. We were speechless. Dumbfounded, to be exact. We didn't know how to react.

Violet broke the awkward silence, "kiss me already Henry." Henry shook his head. She repeated, he didn't budge. "If you kiss me, I will turn into a beautiful woman. The likes of which you have never seen. You can marry me and make everyone around you jealous."

Henry chuckled and said, "at my age, I would rather have a talking frog."

Everyone laughed. Henry was right. Who wouldn't want a talking frog friend?

60

Missing Keys

Marie can admit, she can sometimes be a very forgetful person. There have been times when she forgot to turn off the gas, switch off the fan, and misplaced her glasses. For which, she was often scolded by her husband.

Today is different. Today will not be one of those days. She switched off the fan, turned off the gas, and now that shopping is done, she's going back home.

Now, where did she keep the keys? In her bag? Nope. In her pockets? No luck.

Suddenly, Marie realized. She must have left them in the car. While she frantically headed over to the parking lot, Marie could already hear her husband scolding her. He had scolded her countless times for leaving the keys in the car's ignition, "someone could steal it!" he warned. But who would take that rusty old car?

She looked around the parking lot, only to realize that her husband's fears had come true. The parking lot was empty. Marie was distraught. Now she knew she was in for the scolding of a lifetime. Gathering her courage, she called her husband and told him what happened.

No response. She checked her phone. Did the call get disconnected? No, he was still on the line.

"Honey?"

After a huge sigh, he responded, "what are you talking about, did you forget that I was the one who dropped you off?"

61

The Dentist Appointment

My daughter is a brave girl. When we informed her that she might have to wear braces for a while, she took it like a champ. I am proud of her.

But to my surprise, she was crying her eyes out when she left the appointment. Why? Today was the first day. The dentist was only supposed to make her feel comfortable and tell her what he was going to do. What happened?

She cried, "you never told me I would have to wear braces till I'm 60! I don't want to be stuck with braces for the rest of my life!"

What is she talking about? Curious, I went in to check. There she was, laughing. Grandma Beatrice.

My daughter had asked her, "how long have you been coming here?" And since the clinic belonged to her son, she replied, "all my life."

As for her orthodontic braces, she's only been wearing them for a year now. I couldn't help but chuckle. My daughter got played by Grandma Beatrice.

Catopia

Wait, where am I? Is that a cat? Why is it so close to my face?

"You're finally awake!" the cat cheered. I can only assume this is a dream.

The cat is talking. *The cat is talking*! I must've gone mad. "Sorry, could you please tell me what in the world is going on?" I asked.

"My name is Muffin and we are in Catopia," Muffin looked down at me and waved her paw, a bowl of milk appeared out of thin air. "Go ahead," Muffin said, "make yourself at home, the milk here is amazing!"

It was really good milk. Tipping the bowl back, I emptied the rest into my mouth. "This is great! But why am I—"

"Do you miss Luna?" Muffin interrupted.

Luna was my cat, we had spent 16 wonderful years together before she passed last month. I miss her dearly. "Of course I do. There isn't a day that I don't think about her."

Muffin held out her paw, she said, "Luna wanted to thank you. For taking care of her. For letting her scratch you. And for keeping her well fed all these years," she explained. "She wanted to return the favor."

Tears rolled down my eyes. "I don't know who you are, but thank you! I loved Luna. She was misunderstood but she was the best cat."

Muffin smiled. "As her last wish, Luna has prepared her favorite meal for you," she said. She pointed her paw again, and this time a plate appeared, with a huge, stinky tuna fish laid out on top.

I froze. "No, thank you! The milk was quite filling."

"Aww too bad. Maybe next time then," Muffin looked disappointed, then waved her paw.

I woke up in my bed with a picture of Luna next to me and a fishy scent in the air.

My stomach turned just thinking about next time.

My Favorite Things

Contacts or glasses, and needles for knitting,
A cup of hot tea, close to my sitting,
Bundles of wool, tied up in strings,
These are a few of my favorite things.

Cataracts, Cadillacs, and yoga classes,
Magazines, radios, and false teeth in glasses,
Bundles of newspapers tied up in strings,
These are a few of my favorite things.

When my back creaks, or the kids freak,
When my knees go bad,
I simply remember my favorite things,
And then I don't feel so sad.

The medication I've to take because I'm aging,
Backaches, thin bones, and hair that is thinning,
It might seem unpleasant and sometimes it stings,
But then I remember my favorite things.

Oh yes, my joints ache, and sometimes my hips break,
I might not be able to cut the next cake,
But then I'm reminded of the great life I've had
And then I don't feel so sad.

64

Juries and Aging

Nana turned 80 today. She might look old but she's young at heart. While we were celebrating this huge milestone, my nana received a jury-duty notice. Papa called the clerk's office to remind them that Nana was exempt because of her age.

They replied, "Mrs. Montez needs to come in and fill out the exemption forms."

When Nana told Papa to tell them that she already signed it the previous year, they said, "she has to do it every year."

Nana stood up and walked towards the phone. Taking the receiver from Papa she said, "and why is that, do you really think I am going to get younger?"

65

18 Again

When my boss turned 60, he wasn't really happy. In all honesty, he looked worried.

He did not want his employees to think that he didn't know what was 'hip' today. So, he went ahead and bought a new convertible sports car. But what he was most proud of was his vanity plate. Inscribed on it were the words, "18 again."

A week later, our company welcomed a new employee. He was in his early 20s, making him the youngest employee in our company. My boss really wanted to know what the new guy thought of his new car. When we asked if he came across it, he replied, "oh yeah I did. Who does it belong to?"

With a smirk, my boss replied, "why do you ask?"

The young man responded, "I was wondering why the plate read "I ate again."

No matter how hard you try, there will always be a new 'hip.' And sometimes, that's a good thing.

66

The Emotional Damage

When my husband was bending over to tie our son's shoes, he felt a caress on the back of his head. My husband looked up to see our four-year-old was staring at his hair.

"What is it?" my husband asked.

Gently caressing the slightly thinning spot on my husband's head, with great concern my boy asked, "did you know that you have a hole on your head daddy, does it hurt?"

My husband smiled. He looked down and whispered, "not physically." I tried to hold in my laugh.

67

Flying Pancakes

I was visiting my parents' house after two whole years. And boy, were my parents excited. Not because they were seeing me after a long time, but because they get to spend time with my four-year-old daughter. And of course, show her all the coolest stuff.

As always we were welcomed with the warmest of hugs and the sweetest of smiles. Mom had made all my favorite dishes. Oh, how I missed all this.

While my wife and I were unpacking our bags, my daughter was being entertained by my dad.

I heard my dad say, "want to see something amazing, Ava?" I am assuming Ava said yes because the next thing I hear is Dad loudly telling Mom, who was making pancakes, "let's show her you what we can do Sophia!"

Curious, my wife and I go, only to suddenly see my mom throwing a pancake soaring over her shoulder to dad. And he caught it with a plate! All of us were equally amused. While my dad was standing there, with a proud look on his face, Ava squealed, "more flying pancakes!"

And that is how the flying pancakes routine became a tradition in our house; we could take this act on the road.

68

The Brand New Hat

Sheila was going on her very first cruise. She was so happy that she couldn't hide her excitement. She wanted to try it all but couldn't figure out what she should do first.

Standing by the railing seemed fun. Not only was the view spectacular, but it is a must-do when one is on a cruise. So, there she was, standing near the railing, holding on to her hat.

While she was enjoying the stupendous view she was approached by a young man. Awkwardly he said, "pardon me, miss. I do not mean to sound crude. I felt obliged to inform you that your dress is blowing up in this high wind!"

"I know," she replied. "But both my hands are busy now. While one hand is holding on to the railing, the other is holding on to my hat"

Perplexed and concerned, the youngster replied, "but miss, you must be aware that you are being exposed."

Sheila looked down. Then she looked at the man, dead in the eye, and said, "young man, thank you for your concern but anything you see down there is 70 years old. But this hat, it's brand new. I bought it yesterday!"

69

Sweet Granny Beverly

My dad moved back to his neighborhood after 30 years. He was excited. He couldn't wait to stroll around the park he used to play in and introduce us to all the people he grew up with.

On the first day of moving in, dad jumped up saying, "you guys have to meet Granny Beverly, she is the sweetest. Her pumpkin pies were the best!"

So that evening I went to visit our neighbor, Granny Beverly. We were welcomed by a cute little cat and a grandma whose eyes were dimming. They were also hard of hearing.

She welcomed us with the brightest smile. After settling down, Granny Beverly said, "oh Benjamin, how much you've grown, I've known you since you were a boy, and frankly, you were a huge disappointment."

We were stunned. When my dad was about to say something, she interrupted, "uh-uh let me finish. I was worried sick about you ever since you befriended that good-for-nothing Alfred. Oh, how many times have I advised you to cut ties with him? But you hardly listened. I am glad that you are living with a happy family now.

That must mean you finally cut ties with Alfred. I am proud of you Benjamin."

Everyone went silent. Granny Beverly said, "oh my, why are you being so shy? Here I taste my pumpkin pie, I made it this morning."

After a small pause, my dad stood up and said, "I am sure they taste great. As much as I would love to stay and chat with you, my family and I should go unpack. It was nice catching up with you." And we left.

My dad's name isn't Benjamin. It's Alfred.

70

The Poor Potatoes

Today is a happy day. Not only is Amie going to make my favorite potato stew, but my grandson Luke has offered to help me dig up potatoes. Who could ask for more? Spending time with your grandkids, doing what you love, that right there is a dream come true!

So here we are, digging up potatoes to make potato stew. It sure is sunny today.

"Grandpa!" I could hear Luke call me. I wonder if he's going to love gardening just like I do.

"Yes, Luke?" I turn to see a small child with puffed-up cheeks walking towards me.

Angrily advancing towards me, he says, "Grandpa, I love you." Only to proceed with, "but why did you bury the darn thing in the first place? What did the poor potatoes do to you? Are you evil, Grandpa?"

To Luke's dismay, I burst out laughing. Poor potatoes indeed.

What's My Age Again?

Since we live in different countries, I was visiting my mom after five whole years. While we went for a walk, we bumped into an old family acquaintance.

"Miss Bernard. Hello! Is that your daughter?" the woman asked. "Oh, how much she's grown. How old is she now?"

Without hesitation, my mother replied, "24 years old." Amelia, age 35, wasn't impressed. After saying our goodbyes, I asked my mother, "what was that about? Why did you lie to her?"

She looked away. Then she looked back at me. "Well," she started, "I've been lying about my age for so long, it suddenly dawned on me that I'd have to start lying about yours too."

72

Statistics of Life

Morris turned 103 today. His son, Will, asked him, "Pa, do you think you would be around for your 104th birthday?"

Morris promptly replied, "why of course I would, I even have proof."

"Proof? What proof?" Will asked.

Morris said, "It has been statistically shown that very few people die between the ages of 103 and 104."

He proceeded to give the brightest of smiles. Will was glad that he won't lose Morris anytime soon!

73

The Ultimate Weight Loss Tip

Sarah recently joined a weight loss class. Now, this class has a tradition. At the end of every month, everyone should check their weight and see how much they have progressed.

The person who progressed the most gets a cute medal and a round of applause. Miss Beatrice has been winning the medal for the past four months.

Curious, Sarah went and asked her, "how do you do it?" Cheekily, she responded, "easy, every night I take my teeth out at six o'clock."

That's a Lie

I teach English to primary school children in Taiwan. Frankly, 99% of the time they are the most adorable kids. But sometimes they might tell you something that would most definitely break your heart.

Today, for example, I was teaching them the English tenses. On the board, I wrote, 'I am beautiful.' I proceeded to ask them what tense the sentence was in.

Angela raised her hand.

"Yes, Angela?"

She then asked me, "why are you lying?"

That Unimpressive Hairstyle

It was a hot summer afternoon. My mom and I were visiting the salon to get our hair cut.

Twenty minutes in, and my mom—91 years old—finished having her haircut.

With a huge smile, the stylist announced, "ma'am, not to toot my own horn, but don't you think you look 10 years younger now?"

My mom looked in the mirror. Unimpressed, my mom scoffed and proceeded to tell the stylist, "who would want to look like they are 81 years old?"

76

The Family Cyborg

My daughter couldn't stop staring at my mom cleaning her dentures. It was obvious that she was fascinated.

Seeing my mother carefully taking her dentures out, brushing and rinsing them, only to pop them back in riveted her greatly.

After the procedure, my daughter looked at my mother and said, "you are so cool Grandma, now take off your ear!"

In Loving Memory

When I visited the church this Sunday, I came across my good friend Ally. But something was different today. I noticed my friend Ally wearing a new locket.

Curious, I asked her, "what's in the locket Ally, is it a moment of some sort?" She quickly responded saying, "yes it is, the locket contains a few strands of my husband's hair."

Shocked, I tell her, "but why? Isn't Leroy still alive?"

She chuckled and said, "well of course he is, but his hair isn't."

78

A Grave Encounter

It was Halloween and my son had gone trick-or-treating. When he got back home, he was sweating buckets. I asked him what was wrong and he said he had just come across Mr. Maurice.

He went on to recount the incident After trick-or-treating, he took a shortcut home. While taking the shortcut, he had to cross through the cemetery and when he was halfway across, he heard a loud noise.

"It sounded like someone was breaking something," he recounted. Startled, he went to check for ghosts.

There he spotted instead an old man with a hammer and chisel, chipping away at a headstone.

Relieved, my son approached the man, "I thought you were a ghost, what are you doing working so late?"

"Oh shucks, don't ask," grumbled the old man. "Those idiots, they misspelled my name! Why do they spell Maurice with an O and not with a U?"

79

In the Mood for Love

Clair was in the mood for love. But her husband lying next to her was on the verge of falling asleep.

Clair mumbled under her breath, "I remember how you used to hold my hand all the time." Unenthusiastically her husband reached across, held her hand for a few seconds, and went back to sleep.

After a small pause, Clair mumbled again, "remember how often you used to kiss me?" Now, slightly annoyed, her husband reached across again, gave her a peck on the cheek, and went back to sleep.

After a small pause, Clair went on to say, "remember how you used to bite my cheek right after?" Furiously, he threw his blanket away to get out of bed.

"Where are you going?" Clair asked. Looking at her, he said, "to get my teeth of course!"

A Century of Wisdom

One day, while skimming through the TV channels, I saw a woman being interviewed. She was 104 years old.

The reporter asked, "what is the one thing that you treasure the most?"

Beaming, she replied, "the garden gnome in our backyard that looks a lot like me!"

Surprised, the reporter asked, "what piece of information do you think changed your life?"

Without hesitation, she said, "that the chicken and the ostrich are the closest living relatives of the Tyrannosaurus rex."

Finally, the reporter asked, "what would you say is the best thing about being 104 years old?"

Her reply was simple. She said, "no peer pressure."

81

Precious Moments

My three-year-old granddaughter was about to go to sleep when she said, "Gammy, look!"

She proceeded to show her belly. She said, "look gammy, both you and I have a belly."

"Why yes, we do," I replied.

"Do you have a belly button like me?" she asked, pointing at hers at the same time. After she confirmed that I have one too, she gasped and squealed with excitement saying, "Gammy, I think we are twins!"

Then she took a look at my chest and looked down at hers. Disappointed, she said, "or maybe not." Hiding a smile, I assured her that her chest will also grow once she grows up. Excited, she said, "if I do, then I want them to be purple!"

It's precious moments like these that I live for.

Changes

My husband and I have been married for 30 years. One day we were getting dressed for a party.

I got a haircut, curled my hair, and put on some lipstick. After getting ready, I went to the hall where my husband was sitting. He looked up and said nothing.

Furious, I started complaining about how he didn't notice my hair. I also reminded him of how he used to pay attention to everything before, but now he's just taking me for granted.

And how did he react? He just stood there rubbing his chin while I ranted and raved. Then it hit me: I hadn't noticed that he shaved off his eight-month-old beard.

83

Last Supper

Alanis and Elliot, an elderly couple, were visiting a restaurant that had opened recently.

Because they did not have reservations, they were told that they would have to wait about an hour for a table.

Elliot went over to the manager and told him, "young man, my wife and I are well over 90. Please understand that there is always the possibility of us not having an hour."

They were given a table immediately.

Pure Love

Grandma and Grandpa have been married for 50 years. They are old, funny, adorable, and smart. But you know what I love most about them? Their love for each other.

Grandma always plays with Grandpa, and Grandpa always compliments Grandma. Grandma always burns the food but Grandpa always eats it. He complains of course.

Grandpa gets chased by dogs, but Grandma protects him. Grandma calls him her funny valentine, while Grandpa refers to Grandma as his little star sweeper.

Grandma always listens to Grandpa's rants over the baseball team and Grandpa always listens to Grandma's thoughts on magic.

Grandma and Grandpa always cook for each other and often surprise each other. Of course, they fight, but they always try to make up as soon as possible.

The cherry-on-top? They made an amazing dad and a kind aunt. I love Grandpa and Grandma. They are my role models. I wish to one day be like them!

85

An Absurd Wish

My sister and her husband got married in their late 40s. Thus, they had their kid in their 50s.

One day, my sister and I were talking about how fast the times had passed. It felt like it was only yesterday when we fought over the remote.

My sister sighed and told me, "I can feel my vision dimming, maybe I should go get a pair of glasses."

Immediately after, her kid thundered past us screeching in the loudest voice he could produce.

My sister sighed again, only this time; it was heavier. Then she proceeded to say, "Now, if only I could lose my hearing as well."

86

The Brightside

Distraught over my relentless hair fall, I started ranting to the stylist at the salon, "someday soon, I will stop visiting this salon of yours."

"Oh no, why?" she asked. Nowadays, every time I vacuum, all I pick up is my hair."

The stylist, who was a glass-half-full kind of gal, responded, "well isn't that great then, you can stop vacuuming."

The Moonwalk

My niece was given an assignment where they had to interview senior citizens. They were told to ask these people what was the most historical moment they experienced in their lifetime.

When she asked me the same, I thought for about two minutes and told her, "probably the moonwalk"

She looked at me with utter disappointment. "The most historical thing that happened in your life is Michael Jackson's dance move? I will go ask grandpa."

I'm sorry Neil Armstrong.

88

The Wrong Message

I have a very sweet husband.

He wanted to celebrate my 50th birthday. He invited some old friends of ours to help.

While they were decorating the house and preparing the dishes, my husband left to buy me a gift. Cute little music boxes caught his eyes.

This purple music box was playing "Happy Birthday" Assuming that all the boxes played the same song, he bought a brown box.

After we cut the cake, my husband leaned over, kissed my cheek, and handed me the box. Excited, I opened the box to hear it play, "the old gray mare, she ain't what she used to be."

I had a very sweet husband.

89

Only 70

One day I was talking to my 93-year-old brother. He had recently hurt his back while shoveling snow.

I told him, "you are **93** now, it's about time you pay someone to shovel snow for you."

I could hear my brother grumble. He became all defensive and said, "fiddlesticks! Why would I pay someone to shovel when I can ask my son to do it? He's only 70!"

90

Not Yet

My three-year-old grandson was very curious. One day he asked me, "you are my mom's mom, then who is your mom gramma?"

So I took out an old album and showed him their pictures. Pointing at the pictures, I told him, "this is your great-grandma and this is your great-grandpa."

He looked at me and looked at them. He repeated this gesture a few times. Curious, I asked him, "do I look like them?"

He stared at me and then at the picture. After a two-minute pause, he looked at me and said, "not yet!"

91

Acara

After coming across an ad, my husband had gone and got himself an Amazon Echo.

The ad made him love the device. But after buying it, he found it impossible to activate it. He kept forgetting the name of the device, Alexa.

To help him out, I gave him an idea. Because he is a car fan, I thought he would find it easier if I associated the device with a car. So, I told him, "next time you want to activate it, just think about the car company Lexus. Add an 'a' before its name."

And next time he tried to activate it, I heard him confidently shouting, "Acara, play Frank Sinatra."

92

The Picture

My neighbor recently turned 99, and I was invited to her party. While attending, I took photos of this cheerful yet spunky woman.

I knew she would love to look back on her amazing 99th birthday party. A few days later, I printed the photos and went over to her house.

I showed her the pictures and told her she can keep the ones she loves. She happily accepted my offer and started looking through it. The moment she looked at the picture, she gasped.

"What is it?" I asked.

"Holy fudge! I look like I am 100 in these."

93

Hitch Hiking

One day a police car pulled over at our house. Bewildered, I went to check, only to see my grandpa getting out of the car.

An officer came towards me to explain what was going on. He said, "this old gentleman was lost in the park and asked for help."

After thanking the officer, I went over to Grandpa and asked, "What does he mean you got lost? You've been going there every day for the past 40 years, how could you get lost, grandpa?"

My grandpa smiled slyly, he leaned over to me and said, "I didn't get lost. I just got tired of walking."

Life: The Four Stages

Stage 1: You believe in Santa Claus and you can't wait to meet him.

Stage 2: You're the cool, mature kid who knows that Santa isn't real. And you make sure that every child, parent, and grandparent around you knows that you don't believe in Santa!

Stage 3: You find yourself buying that Santa wig because you are about to be your child's Santa. Can't wait to eat those cookies later!

Stage 4: Children come and ask you if you are Santa. They usually either tell you their Christmas wishes or cry because you didn't get them the latest game console last Christmas.

And those are the four stages of life!

95

Tuesdays Only

My grandson came running and asked me, "Gammy, even if Mumma doesn't support my dream job, you will, right?"

How can I say no to him? I say, "of course, I will, but now I'm curious. What is it that you want to be?"

With a stern face, he said, "a garbage man."

Surprised, I asked him, "and why do you want to be a garbage man?"

His face lit up as he said, "obviously because they only work on Tuesdays!"

Kids, am I right?

Words of Wisdom

Certain events lead to my daughter-in-law being sad. Not only was her boss overworking her and not giving her the promotion she deserves, her wallet along with her phone was missing.

After looking everywhere and tearing out a handful of hairs, she started crying.

Now I wasn't sure what to do or how to console her, but while I was fretting about it, my grandson came to my rescue.

The three-year-old went over to his mother and patted her head. Then he said, "don't cry Mom, sometimes toys break, and batteries die."

97

Marriage

One day, my granddaughter told me, "When I grow up, I will marry you, grandpa." Her older brother looked her in the eye and said, "you can't marry your own grandfather."

"Oh? Then I will marry daddy." Her brother, now annoyed, told her, "you can't marry your own father!"

Disappointed, she said, "I guess I will marry you then."

Now furious, he said, "eww, you can't marry me!"

On the verge of tears, she asked, "does no one here love me?"

Calmly, I explained, "of course we love you sweetheart, but you can't marry someone in your own family."

She burst into tears and asked, "you mean I have to marry a complete stranger?"

98

Hippy Grandma

Last week my two-year-old nephew asked me, "what's a hipster?"

Trying to explain it as simply as possible, I said, "a hipster is someone who wears unique clothes and thick glasses."

As his eyes widened, he exclaimed, "so Grandma is a hipster?"

99

That Cool Hairstyle

I had accompanied my baby niece to the mall. After roaming around the mall for about 40 minutes, we sat down to rest.

And for some reason, I could sense that I was being watched. And more often than not, the people looking at me were women.

This made me feel more macho than ever, it made me feel great. I—a 50-year-old man—was being eyed by women in a shopping mall. I must be one handsome dude.

While getting up, I ran my fingers through my hair, trying to look cool for my new fans.

It was then that I discovered two pink hair clips artfully placed on my head. Well, at least my niece had a future in hairstyling.

Get Well Soon

After having been retired for two years, staying home every day was really starting to bore me. I couldn't think of a single thing to do.

That was when I thought, if I'm this bored, after only two years, I wonder how bored people who live in retirement homes are.

Thus, I took it upon myself to visit retirement homes and entertain the people who lived there. The first retirement home I went to was great!

While I was there I played games, sang songs, and narrated funny stories. Everyone was laughing and clapping along. I knew it! I knew this would turn out to be a success, I knew they needed me.

And just as I was saying my goodbyes and getting ready to leave, the people gathered around and shouted, "get well soon!"

Conclusion

Well, this is it, after so many hilarious stories your stomach is bound to be aching. Now that you've reached the end of this journey, are you noticing any improvements in your mind and memory? Did they trigger any old memories of good times? I sure hope so.

Just remember, getting old isn't always easy and you are bound to face a lot of hardships, but it is a gift. Look at you! You are living a long and happy life. You get to see your friends and family grow and live. You get to experience new things and make new memories with old friends. You can wear whatever you want, and you don't have to care about what others think. You can discover a new romance or travel to places you've never been to before.

There is still so much of your amazing life to live. Make sure to see the funny side of life's challenges and focus on the moments that bring you joy. And don't forget, you have so many great stories to tell.

Do come back to this book when you feel like reliving your glory days, or just when you want a good laugh. I mean, who wouldn't want to relive salon disasters or holiday hiccups with a hearty chuckle?